HAPPY
SURPRISES

Chris,
Happy Surprise to you!
Dave

HELP OTHERS DISCOVER
THE JOY OF GIVING

DAVID L. HEETLAND

Happy Surprises: Help Others Discover the Joy of Giving

The General Board of Higher Education and Ministry leads and serves The United Methodist Church in the recruitment, preparation, nurture, education, and support of Christian leaders—lay and clergy—for the work of making disciples of Jesus Christ for the transformation of the world. Its vision is that a new generation of Christian leaders will commit boldly to Jesus Christ and be characterized by intellectual excellence, moral integrity, spiritual courage, and holiness of heart and life. The General Board of Higher Education and Ministry of The United Methodist Church serves as an advocate for the intellectual life of the church. The Board's mission embodies the Wesleyan tradition of commitment to the education of laypersons and ordained persons by providing access to higher education for all persons.

Wesley's Foundery Books is named for the abandoned foundery that early followers of John Wesley transformed, which later became the cradle of London's Methodist movement.

HIGHER EDUCATION & MINISTRY
General Board of Higher Education and Ministry
THE UNITED METHODIST CHURCH

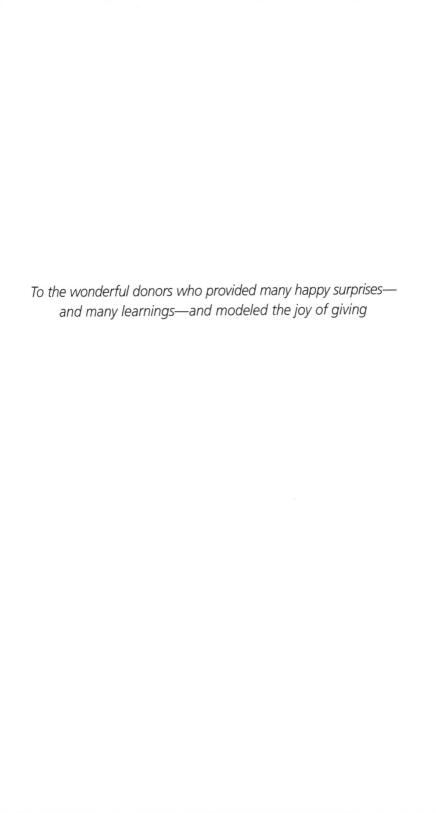

*To the wonderful donors who provided many happy surprises—
and many learnings—and modeled the joy of giving*

Contents

Acknowledgments

My life has been greatly enriched by the hundreds of donors I have met over the years who have shared their stories with me, including stories of discovering the joy of giving.

In addition to the many generous donors I have been blessed to know, I have also been privileged to work with wonderful colleagues. I am deeply grateful to Jim Beddow for inviting me to head up the development office at Dakota Wesleyan University many years ago, even though I had no formal training in fundraising at that time. I am grateful for the opportunity I've had to work with four fine presidents at Garrett-Evangelical (Neal Fisher, Ted Campbell, Phil Amerson, and Lallene Rector), all who gave me the freedom to do what I felt needed to be done to build a strong development program, and for my dedicated development staff colleagues (too numerous to mention). I am also grateful for the friendship and mentorship I've received over the years from several development consultants (Chuck Kayton, Russ Weigand, Bill Hausman,

Ron Gunden, and Ted Grossnickle). Just as I have learned much from donors over the years, so too have I learned much from each of these colleagues.

I chuckle when I remember sharing with Neal Fisher some of my memorable visits with donors. He would always respond by saying, "Another chapter for your book someday." Well, Neal, here is that book at last! And it's a more coherent book because of the helpful suggestions made by Neal Fisher, Jim Beddow, Ted Campbell, Russ Weigand, Bill Hausman, Ron Gunden, and William Enright, who graciously read and critiqued my manuscript. Thank you all for your encouragement and support.

Thanks also to Kathryn Armistead, publisher for Wesley's Foundery Books, who was most helpful in bringing this book to life. It has been a joy to work with you on this project.

Finally, special thanks to Kathy Heetland, my strongest supporter and my proofreader. You know that I always value your insights and your patience. Thanks for being there when I need you—and for leaving me alone when I am deep into writing.

Preface

Jim Beddow, then president of Dakota Wesleyan University in Mitchell, South Dakota, invited me into his office one day many years ago and asked me to head up the development office. At the time I was serving as dean of student services and had earlier served as campus minister and assistant professor of religion and philosophy at the university. I knew what the joys of campus ministry were—helping students discover their callings in life. I knew what the joys of teaching were—helping students discover new insights about the world and themselves. And I knew what the joys of being dean of student services were—creating an environment and programs that complemented the academic program and fostered the development of the whole person. But I could not imagine what the joys would be in fundraising.

"Why would I want to do that?" I asked, incredulously. My image of a fundraiser was somewhat akin to a slick, fast-talking salesperson trying to sell a bill of goods. I can still remember

Jim's response, all these years later. "Lawyers work with people who have problems," he said, "and doctors work with people who are ill. Fundraisers, however, get to work with the very best people who are at their best." He went on to say, "Fundraisers get to be matchmakers—bringing together the dreams of individuals and the goals of an organization."

He convinced me to give it a try—and soon after, I had my first happy surprise: he was right! There was true joy in meeting, and working with, some wonderful people, people of vision who wanted to make a positive difference in the world. Bringing together their dreams and the mission of the university was a richly rewarding experience.

A year later I had the opportunity to join the development team at Garrett-Evangelical Theological Seminary in Evanston, Illinois. While I hated to leave Dakota Wesleyan University, I was excited about the opportunity to work in a seminary setting since seminary had been such a formative part of my own life. I knew I had passion for the mission of a graduate theological school that prepares skilled, bold, and articulate leaders for churches and communities around the world.

It has been an exhilarating adventure, filled with many happy surprises, including three successful capital campaigns that exceeded their goals and many other fundraising projects. After serving as vice president for development at Garrett-Evangelical for thirty-five years, I told the president it was time for someone else to have the fun of managing the next capital campaign so I could focus on helping people with their charitable estate planning. Today, as senior vice president for planned giving, I continue to find joy in bringing together the dreams of individuals and the mission of Garrett-Evangelical.

I can also recall the words of another person, upon learning that I was moving into fundraising. "You will discover," he said, "that fundraising is a series of disappointments, interspersed with a few happy surprises." While it is true that fundraising has its share of disappointments, I have found that the happy surprises far outnumber the disappointments. Indeed, it is these happy surprises—never knowing for sure who will make a significant gift, or when, or why—that have kept me motivated all these years.

Some years ago, I began ending each development report to the board of trustees by sharing a story of a happy surprise and what we could learn from that gift. Board members looked forward to these stories. Some would even ask at the beginning of a board meeting, "Do you have a happy surprise to share with us today?" More often than not, the answer was "Yes!"

A number of people suggested that others might learn from these stories as well. Therefore, I have collected some of the more memorable happy surprises to share. I hope they will encourage and inspire development officers, presidents, trustees, and volunteers to see fundraising not as a necessary evil, but rather as a joyful opportunity. I also hope these stories will inspire others to discover the joy of giving, just as these donors have.

At the end of each chapter, there is a section for you to make notes and jot down your own plans and names of prospective donors.

Enjoy!

Keys to Successful Fundraising

The Power of Passion

I believe the keys to successful fundraising are passion, persistence, and patience. Let's take a look at the first key: passion.

If you are passionate about the mission of your organization and you share your passion with others, it will be contagious. If you don't feel passionate about your organization's mission, perhaps you need to ask yourself if you are in the right place.

How do you develop passion for your organization's mission? Hopefully you

> **The three keys to successful fundraising: passion, persistence, and patience.**

have chosen to work or volunteer at an organization whose mission and values are closely aligned with your own. Thus, it should be easy to talk with enthusiasm about what your organization is accomplishing—and what more it could accomplish with appropriate funding.

One of the best ways to demonstrate that passion is to make your own gift before you invite anyone else to give to your organization. When we were launching our first capital campaign a number of years ago, the campaign consultant told us that the first two commitments needed to come from the president and the vice president for development. If we weren't committed, he said, why should we expect others, who aren't as close to the institution, to be committed? "If you want to challenge others to make transformative gifts," he said, "first challenge yourselves to make transformative gifts!" After making our own commitments, he noted, we would be in a much better position to speak passionately with others about our goals for the seminary.

Passion is contagious.

I found his words to be right on target. If we make our own commitment before we invite others to make theirs, we will be able to speak with passion, enthusiasm, and integrity. And we will be able to say, "Will you join me in supporting these goals?"

It doesn't happen often, but I once had a prospective donor ask me what my own commitment was to the capital campaign that I was inviting him to consider. Gary was a young man who was interested in our organization, but he didn't have unlimited resources, and he had other charitable interests as well as family obligations. "What are you personally giving to the campaign?" he asked me pointedly. I shared with him the commitment I had made. He later told me he was inspired to do more than he had originally planned when he learned that I

You must be personally *and* financially invested in your cause.

was not just a "hired hand" but was personally invested in the campaign in a significant way.

What can we learn from this happy surprise? Actions speak louder than words, and if we make our own commitment before inviting others to make theirs, we will be able to speak with passion, enthusiasm, and integrity.

Notes

The Power
of Persistence

The second key to successful fundraising is persistence. Major gifts are rarely received on the first (or even second or third) visit, so you must persist and continue to nurture those relationships—sometimes over a long period of time—in spite of challenges and setbacks.

Sharon is a good example. Her pastor had given me her name, saying she was a very active member of his church, and he thought she would be interested in learning more about the seminary. I called her on the phone to arrange an appointment and found her to be pleasant and open to a visit. However, she indicated that she was busy for the next several weeks and asked that I call her back in a month to schedule an appointment, which I did. Once again, the timing was not right for her, and

To receive gifts, you need to nurture donor relationships over time.

she asked me to call her back "a little later." And so it went, for over a year. She always seemed pleasant and genuinely interested in learning more, but she always had one reason or another why we couldn't meet. I began to wonder if I was wasting my time—and hers!

Finally, after more than a year of trying to schedule a visit, we found a day and time that worked for both of us. I drove the three hours to her home and had a delightful two-hour visit, during which I learned about her family, the family business, her church involvements, and her appreciation for several of our graduates whom she knew and respected, including her pastor.

I walked Sharon through the seminary's campaign case statement. She commented that my visit was timely, as she and her husband (who went to a different church) were just beginning to discuss their estate plans and that their major charitable giving would be done through their estate. She thought the seminary might be a good place to receive some of their money, but she wanted to get to know us better.

When I invited her to the campus to get better acquainted, she was immediately open to the idea. She said she liked to come to the Chicago area and would be driving through in a few weeks on her way to Florida. If that time didn't work, she would look for another time in the near future to visit.

Then the real test of persistence began. It did not work out for her to visit the campus on her way to Florida—or in the weeks following. In fact, despite repeated invitations, it did not work out for her for five more years! I was able to visit her in her home a few more times in those intervening years, but each time she expressed interest in getting to know the seminary better through a personal visit.

And then it happened. She came to the campus for a day. She toured the grounds, participated in the chapel service, met some faculty and staff, and had lunch with several students. At the end of the day, she commented, "Now I understand what you have tried to tell me in your visits. This is an exciting place!"

Shortly thereafter we received the following note from her:

> Thank you for a wonderful and inspirational day at Garrett-Evangelical. I am so happy I finally was able to see the campus and experience some of the enthusiasm existing there. I appreciate your efforts in making my visit a very special day. Sincerely, Sharon.

And not too long after that, we received notification that Sharon and her husband had included the seminary in their estate plans for a $100,000 unrestricted gift.

What can we learn from this happy surprise? Persistence pays!

 Notes

The Power of Patience

3

The third key to successful fundraising is patience. While passion and persistence are essential for any fundraiser, what is equally important is to practice patience (or as I sometimes say, "patient urgency") because gifts are made on the donor's time schedule, not ours.

Ernie taught me the power of patience. He was the lead donor in our $35 million capital campaign. When that goal was reached three years later, the trustees raised the goal to $60 million. Ernie again stepped forward with another lead gift. When the $60 million goal was surpassed three years later, the trustees again raised the goal—this time to $100 million—to address some still-unmet needs as well as some new opportunities.

So naturally Ernie was the first person I went to visit after the trustees raised the goal for the second time. I told him that the board of trustees had voted unanimously to increase the campaign goal to $100 million and that the board chair had asked me to share with Ernie our hopes that he would help set the pace for this expanded campaign with another lead gift. I walked him through the new case statement and reviewed several areas in our expanded campaign that he might want to consider. I told him he was the only donor I knew who had the capability of being our lead donor.

Ernie responded by saying that this had been the worst year for his business in more than twenty-five years, and he was not able to make an additional commitment. He suggested that we keep in touch and said that perhaps next year would be different. He then looked me in the eye and said, "Let's just say I will give you a definite maybe." I told him a "definite maybe" was much better than a "definite no," and I could live with that. I then thanked him for what he had already done in the first two phases of the campaign and told him we were extremely grateful for

A "definite maybe" is better than a "definite no."

his generosity. He responded that he was glad he could do it, and said, "I won't forget the seminary."

Each year, for the next six years, I visited him and asked him if he was ready to turn his "definite maybe" into a "definite yes." And each time his answer was no. Then he would smile and say, "Don't give up hope."

Patience is not passive waiting but active hope.

By the seventh year we were no longer looking for a pacesetting gift, but a gift to complete the campaign. So, I asked him if he would consider a major gift to put the campaign over the top. To my happy surprise, he said he would consider it! A few weeks later I received a phone call with the good news that a gift intention form was in the mail, confirming his commitment to put the campaign over the top!

What can we learn from this happy surprise? This gift required passion, persistence, and a lot of patience—seven years' worth of patience. But it was well worth the wait, as Ernie was indeed the lead donor in our $100 million campaign. Persist in telling your organization's story with passion—and then practice patience (or patient urgency)!

Notes

Steps to Successful Fundraising

The Importance of Cultivation—The Short Version

4

Just as there are three keys to successful fundraising (passion, persistence, and patience), there are also three steps to successful fundraising: cultivation, invitation, and saying "Thank you."

The first step, cultivation, seeks to develop meaningful relationships with donors, built on trust and mutual respect. The goal of the cultivation process is to understand donors in their fullness—their values and goals—and to discover where their interests and the mission of your organization intersect. Cultivation may take a day, or it may take several years. First, an example of the short version:

> **Three steps of successful fundraising: cultivation, invitation, and saying "Thank you."**

On April 13 I was preparing our trustee development committee agenda, and I wondered how I could include a happy surprise on the agenda. None immediately came to mind. Then the phone rang. (I am not making this up!)

A woman on the other end said she was interested in making a stock gift and wanted to know how to do so. I told her I would be happy to email her the instructions on how to transfer the stock electronically. She said that wouldn't be possible because she had an actual stock certificate. I hadn't seen an actual stock certificate in years; today almost all stock gifts are transferred electronically.

I explained she needed to mail the certificate and an irrevocable stock power form in separate envelopes. She stopped me and said, "I was hoping you would come by and pick up the certificate. I'm sure you must get my way all the time." I told her I didn't get there as often as I would like, but I could arrange for that to happen. "Well, can we look at our calendars and find a date this week?" she asked. And so, two days later I was on my way to her home.

Upon arrival, I met a sharp ninety-two-year-old woman named Betty. After getting acquainted, I told her we would need to have a third-party release form signed by a notary. So, off we went to find a notary and get that form signed.

Next, we needed to go to her bank and have her sign the stock certificate in front of her trust officer, who could guarantee her signature. When her trust officer looked up her records, he told her she didn't actually own 1,116 shares of SBC stock (as the stock certificate indicated) but rather 2,232 shares of AT&T stock. Did she want to give the seminary 1,116 shares or 2,232 shares?

There was a long pause as she thought about this—and I fervently prayed. Then she said, "I want to give it all to the seminary—but how can I do so, since the stock certificate is only for 1,116 shares of SBC stock?"

That led to several long-distance phone calls and learning that she could transfer all 2,232 shares of AT&T stock to the seminary electronically if she filled out forms that could be downloaded from the Internet. With the trust officer's assistance, we downloaded the forms and spent the next hour filling them out and getting his signature guarantee. Then it was off to the post office to get those forms in the mail as quickly as possible. However, remember that this was April 15, so quick was not the operative word at the post office on that particular day. Nor would it be the word I would use to describe how a ninety-two-year-old woman with a walker moves. Nonetheless, we got the forms mailed before the post office closed.

On the way back to her home, Betty mentioned that we would be passing by her health clinic and she wondered if we could stop there so she could take care of some business. Of course! As we neared her home at last, she looked at me and said, "I think this has been a good day for both of us." I wholeheartedly agreed!

By the way, her gift of stock was valued at $73,000. She used it to establish a gift annuity, with the proceeds earmarked to fund a scholarship in her name. Since the annuity paid 9 percent for as long as she lived, it was indeed a good day for her. Because the seminary got a new scholarship, it was also a very good day for us. And I had a happy surprise to share at the next board meeting after all!

Listen to the donor, and let the donor lead the way.

What can we learn from this happy surprise? Listen to the donor, and let the donor lead the way in the cultivation process. By listening to Betty's goals and learning about her interests and her sense of urgency, I was able to move the cultivation process along very quickly—even if it was a long day!

Notes

The Importance of Cultivation—The Long Version

5

Some happy surprises happen quickly and unexpectedly. More often, however, they happen after a long time of cultivation. Let me share two happy surprises that belong in that latter category.

In 1995 Glen, one of our graduates, informed me that he had included the seminary in his will. This was the beginning of our relationship.

We kept in touch with each other, and in 2004 he reaffirmed his planned gift commitment but indicated he couldn't even guess what the amount would be.

We continued to keep in touch, and in 2008 he again affirmed his commitment and estimated the value of his gift to be $5,000.

Then, in 2011, he shared with me that he had a lake cabin in Michigan that he felt it was time to get rid of since he was now eighty-five, and he wanted to explore the possibility of gifting it to the seminary. These conversations continued for the next three years!

In May 2014 he said he felt the time was right to gift this property to the seminary, as he was no longer able to take care of it, but first he needed to have some repair work done.

In May 2015 he indicated he was finally ready to move forward. However, when you're eighty-nine years old, you don't move forward quickly. Nonetheless, conversations continued through the summer as he sought appraisals for the property, had the necessary inspections, and prepared the property to be marketable. By then, the summer was over, and it was time to lock it up for the winter.

Conversations resumed in the spring of 2016—and then the happy surprise happened! On July 28, 2016, Glen really did transfer the property he had bought many years ago for $25,000 to the seminary. That same day we sold it to his neighbors, who had been patiently waiting to buy it, for $135,000. Oh, and by the way, we are still in his will!

That's Glen's story. And here is Glenna's story:

Glenna attended a small informational gathering hosted by two of our trustees in 2004. She accepted their invitation "with gratitude for the opportunity to learn more about the seminary." Following the gathering, I visited her in her home to receive her feedback and invite her support. She said she wanted to do something for the seminary but could not make a major commitment at that time since she had just stretched herself to make a three-year commitment to her church renovation project. Once that was completed, she said, she would be willing to consider a larger commitment to the seminary. In the meantime, she gave me a check for $100.

Thus began the cultivation process. We visited from time to time, she received our mailings, and she made occasional gifts of $100.

In September 2009 Glenna called to say that she was including the seminary in her will but was not able to do anything more during her lifetime and requested to be taken off the mailing list. In this case, cultivation meant honoring her request and simply touching base with her from time to time by phone.

Glenna passed away in September 2015, and some months later we received an estate gift of $113,520. A happy surprise from a faith-ful $100 donor.

> **Often major gifts come about after years of cultivation, nurturing, and practicing patience.**

What can we learn from these two happy surprises? While the cultivation process sometimes happens quickly, as it did with Betty, more often major gifts come about after years of cultivation, nurturing, and practicing patience, as was the case with both Glen and Glenna.

Notes

The Importance of Invitation

6

The second step to successful fundraising is invitation, or inviting a gift. I prefer the term *invitation* rather than *solicitation*. We are inviting individuals to become our partners in a worthy endeavor. We are not accosting them and trying to convince them to do something they don't want to do. It is our task to extend the invitation. It is their task to determine whether or not to accept our invitation.

> **It is our task to extend the invitation. It is their task to determine whether or not to accept our invitation.**

One of the first people I met when I began working at the seminary was Luella, a remarkably spry and delightful ninety-two-year-old, with a good sense of humor. Luella had made a nice gift to the seminary some years earlier, but nothing in recent years. I wanted to meet her, thank her for her gift, and invite her to consider another one.

Luella had been widowed for twenty-four years. She lived alone on her 720-acre farm. Although she had a farm manager, she remained actively involved in the decision-making. Her other major interest was her small, rural church. After learning about her life on the farm, I brought her up to date on the seminary and invited her renewed support. She said her cash flow was tight at the moment and she could not give much. She then proceeded to write a check for $1,000, calling it "chicken feed." She seemed open to doing more once she knew better what her financial situation would be in the year ahead.

When I visited her again a few months later, we picked up the conversation where we'd last left off. Luella indicated that she had a $10,000 CD that she was considering gifting to the seminary through her will.

I then asked her what would happen to her farm when she passed away. "Oh, that's all taken care of," she said with a smile. She then explained that the farm would be placed in trust upon her death, with her church receiving the income from the farm in perpetuity.

The time seemed right to extend an invitation. "That's wonderful that you want to remember your church," I said. "Another way to ensure that your church stays strong is to make sure it has strong leadership. Perhaps you would want to consider gifting part of the farm income to the seminary to help train future ministers." That was the extent of my invitation. Then it was time to head home, with a fresh loaf of sourdough bread from her oven.

When I visited her again several weeks later, she met me at the door with a big smile. "Well, I did it!" she said, beaming.

"Did what?" I asked.

"I changed my will, so the seminary will receive half of the income from my farm. The other half will go to my church." She was pleased to know that her farm income would strengthen not only her local church but also churches throughout the country through well-trained ministers.

Luella passed away a year and a half later. The seminary continues to receive between $10,000 and $20,000 each year in farm income—all because we invited Luella to join us in this worthy endeavor of preparing strong leaders for our churches and communities.

Share your passion for the mission of your organization, and invite others to join you in supporting its work!

What can we learn from this happy surprise? Share your passion for the mission of your organization—and don't forget to invite others to join you in supporting its work!

Notes

The Importance of "Thank You"

7

Early in my fundraising career, a wise mentor shared with me the reason for her success. "When someone makes a gift, I just keep thanking him or her until they make the next gift," she said with a smile. I soon discovered the wisdom of her words.

As I began my work at the seminary, I reviewed the names of previous donors. I noted that a woman named Alice had made a nice gift of $10,000 a few years earlier to establish a scholarship in memory of her father. According to her file, no one had ever visited her and thanked her personally for her gift. *Better late than never,* I thought, so I called her on the phone and told her I would like to come and visit her. "There is no need to do that," she responded. "That was a onetime gift, and I can't do anything more." I persisted, saying I was going to be in her community anyway and just wanted to stop by and personally thank her for her generosity. She finally relented and agreed that I could stop by as long as I did not ask her for another gift. I promised I would not.

On the day of the visit, I reminded myself that my sole purpose for the visit was to thank her for her gift in memory of her father. And that is what I did. I thanked her for remembering her father by starting a scholarship in his name. She told me she had done so because her father had once thought of becoming a minister himself. Instead he had gone into business and had done well. The church had remained a vital part of his life, however, and he'd recognized the importance of well-trained ministers. In fact, he'd supported the seminary over the years with annual gifts. That is what led Alice to establish a scholarship at the seminary in his name at the time of his death.

"By the way, how large is that scholarship?" she asked. When I told her the amount in the endowment fund, she was surprised at how small it was. She commented that she had a grandchild in law school, so she was well aware of the cost of higher education.

"That scholarship needs to be larger," she said, noting that it didn't begin to cover the cost of tuition. I assured her that every scholarship, no matter how small, was making a difference. She apologized for her lack of recent support, saying what she had done in the past was very limited and she needed to do more.

There is power in saying "Thank you."

That thank-you visit resulted in Alice resuming her annual support to her father's scholarship. It was also the first of many other visits to her home. Each year I would visit her, thank her for her continued leadership support, and bring her a thank-you letter from that year's student recipient. And each year she would affirm her commitment to continue growing the scholarship. She eventually shared that she had included the seminary in her estate planning as well—all because we took the time to say, "Thank you."

What can we learn from this happy surprise? You can never say "Thank you" too many times! And doing so may well lead to future gifts.

You can never say "Thank you" too many times.

Notes

Components of Successful Fundraising

Encourage
Annual Gifts

8

Just as there are three keys to successful fundraising (passion, persistence, and patience) and three steps to successful fundraising (cultivation, invitation, and thank you), so too there are three essential components of fundraising: annual gifts, capital gifts, and planned gifts.

A strong fundraising program seeks regularly to encourage these three avenues of giving. While there is not a specific order in which these gifts are encouraged, many donors begin by making annual gifts, followed perhaps with occasional capital gifts during capital campaigns, and finally, a planned gift commitment when donors do their estate planning.

> The three components of fundraising: annual gifts, capital gifts, and planned gifts.

Ron and Sara are perfect examples of this sequence of giving. Ron graduated from the seminary. Upon graduation, he followed a different path from most seminary graduates. He went to work for IBM, a career that lasted until he retired. "Perhaps my seminary education was not as directly applicable to my vocation as with most graduates," he noted, "but I was an enlightened member of every congregation where I was involved. Indeed, I still believe that everyone should have at least two years of seminary education."

It is clear that Ron remains very grateful for his seminary training. He and Sara have been faithful leadership donors to the seminary's annual fund for many years. "Gifting benefits us more than we realize," Ron notes. "We will continue to do so as long as we are able."

In addition to their annual leadership gifts, Ron and Sara were major donors to the seminary's Forging Our Future campaign, establishing an endowed scholarship in their names and making significant gifts to unrestricted endowment as well.

Publicize and encourage the three components on a regular basis.

Because of their faithful annual and capital giving, it should be no surprise to learn that they also take planned giving seriously. They have done this in two ways. First, they have taken out thirteen gift annuities in recent years, for a total of more than $645,000.

They have also included the seminary in their wills. Ron explains why: "We were once told by a financial planner that as parents we should spend our money on what we want rather than leave it to our kids, because we will not like the way they spend it. I would not go that far, but there is some truth to that. So that is why we have included the seminary in our wills."

What can we learn from Ron and Sara? It is a happy surprise when donors take seriously the three components of fundraising by making annual gifts, capital gifts, and planned gifts to our organizations. We significantly increase the likelihood of similar happy surprises if we make sure that these three avenues of giving are properly publicized and encouraged on a regular basis.

Notes

Encourage Capital Gifts

9

Sometimes the first gift a donor makes is a capital gift, often in response to a special appeal or capital campaign.

This was the case for Rob. When one of our alums, a beloved pastor, was retiring, the seminary chose to honor him by establishing a scholarship in his name and inviting members of the congregation to add to the scholarship. Rob, an active member of the congregation, responded to the invitation by sending a check for $10,000—a very happy surprise!

I immediately thanked Rob for this wonderful gift and told him I'd love to find a time to stop by and thank him personally, bring him up to date on the scholarship, and simply have a chance to meet him. Rob agreed to meet at a coffee shop near his office a few weeks later.

It was a great first visit. I learned about Rob's family, his business, and his church and civic involvements. When I asked what prompted his generous gift, he said it was his appreciation for their pastor's ministry. I asked whether he would be open to further involvement with the seminary. He said, "Yes, I would be open to that, as long as you are aware of my other work, family, and civic commitments." He said he would first enjoy visiting the campus.

Because of his busy schedule, it took nearly a year before Rob was able to visit campus. He attended chapel and then had lunch with the president and me, followed by a tour of the campus. Throughout the visit he asked thoughtful questions and seemed interested in learning more about the seminary. At the conclusion of the visit, I told him I hoped that this was the first of many visits and that we could find ways to involve him more deeply in the life of the seminary. He seemed open to that possibility.

That was indeed the first of many visits and conversations. We invited Rob to consider joining the board of trustees. He was open to the idea but said the timing wasn't right in light of some other major responsibilities at church and at work. He did, however, begin supporting our annual fund with a $5,000 gift.

Three years after that first visit to the campus, Rob joined the board of trustees. Shortly thereafter, he made a $100,000 unrestricted commitment to the seminary's Forging Our Future capital campaign. And a year later he became chair of the trustee's development committee. He has indicated a willingness to consider a planned gift commitment in the future as well.

Thank the person for that gift, learn what motivated the gift, and begin a relationship-building process that connects the person's interests with the organization's mission.

What can we learn from Rob? It doesn't matter if a person's first gift is an annual gift, a capital gift, or a planned gift. What matters is making sure that we properly thank the person for that gift, that we learn what motivated the gift, and that we begin a relationship-building process that connects the person's interests with the organization's mission. If we can do that, we just might experience some happy surprises!

Notes

Encourage Planned Gifts

10

While it does not happen often, sometimes the first gift to an organization is a planned gift. Orpha's is such an example.

Like many couples, Orpha and her husband, John, discussed their wills and their wishes for charitable bequests at times during their marriage. They agreed that they wanted to help people in need and support projects that reflected their values. However, it was not until after John died that Orpha realized their wills did not leave anything to charity. She decided it was time to act on their intentions.

"Since John's passing, I have become aware that life is fragile, and it is good to have things in place," Orpha said. "We agreed it is important to remember charity as well as family."

Orpha wanted to be sure she made the right choices in leaving a legacy, so she started attending seminars and seeking professional advice on the best way to leave contributions to worthy causes. She learned that, in addition to leaving a bequest in one's will, one can create a charitable trust, purchase a gift annuity, or buy a life insurance policy that names the charity as beneficiary. "My financial planner is well versed in insurance, so we chose a life insurance plan," noted Orpha. "The good thing is that you can determine a premium that fits your budget, and that determines the amount of the policy."

Having determined how to give, Orpha next set out to determine where to give. The church has been an important part of her life ever since she was a little girl. Today she is retired from a career in banking, and the church remains an essential part of her life.

Over the years Orpha realized that many of her pastors were graduates of our seminary. She was also aware that our students served as interns at her church. So, she called me one day to learn about the seminary's needs and goals.

> We need to tell the stories of our organization whenever and wherever we can.

I met with Orpha and her financial planner and told them about the various goals of the seminary's $100 million campaign. Orpha knew that many students struggled financially to get through seminary. Thus, she was immediately attracted to the goal of providing more scholarship support to our students. When she learned that she could establish an endowed scholarship in her and John's names, she and her financial planner agreed this was a wonderful way to leave a legacy.

"I determined that the seminary would be the owner and beneficiary of the policy," Orpha stated. "I am paying the premium by sending my check to the seminary, which creates a tax benefit by making an annual charitable contribution. It is like giving an annual gift that will later on provide scholarship assistance to some deserving student."

Orpha smiled and then said, "In spite of the fact that the seminary is anxious to award more scholarships, David has assured me that he is praying for my longevity! In fact, he helped me to see that I could assist students now as well as in the future." Orpha is doing this by making an annual gift, in addition to the insurance premium, which is awarded each year as an annual scholarship in her and John's names. Orpha was thrilled to receive a thank-you letter from her first scholarship recipient.

After she finalized her charitable estate plans, Orpha wrote about the seminary in the church newsletter, shared in church what she had done, and encouraged others to consider doing likewise.

"It gives me a great sense of satisfaction to know I am leaving a legacy that reflects my values, and that students in the future will be able to pursue their call to ministry because of this scholarship," said Orpha. "I hope others will consider what legacy they want to leave."

What can we learn from Orpha? There are many others like her who are looking for institutions that share their values. They may not be current donors, but they are open to learning more. Thus, we need to tell our stories whenever and wherever we can if we want to receive a happy surprise like this!

Notes

Where to Start

Start with Those Who Know You Best

11

A wise mentor once said to me, "Don't look for wealthy people and hope they will become your friends. Rather, look to your friends and hope that some of them have wealth." Those words have served me very well over the years, reminding me that our best donors are often those closest to our organization. In the seminary setting, that means faculty, staff, and even students. While they may not have great wealth, they share our passion for the seminary's mission and are often willing to make significant gifts to further our work.

Dorothy is a shining example of that truth. She worked at the seminary for fourteen years in an administrative role before taking early retirement. When asked to recall her most vivid memories, Dorothy spoke of the commitment, talent, and leadership of two presidents she worked with; the chapel services, with beautiful organ and vocal music and inspiring sermons; and, of course, the students.

"The students made a strong impression upon me," she said, "as I saw the sacrifices they made to come to seminary, how many of them struggled to make ends meet, and their deep dedication and commitment to their callings."

Thus, when the seminary announced its 150th anniversary capital campaign in 2003, Dorothy knew she wanted to be a part of it. When asked why, Dorothy responded, "I believe in the mission and purpose of the school; in the committed administration, faculty, and staff; and especially in the students. I chose to establish a scholarship fund because I saw the students struggle, saw how much financial aid meant to them, and realized they were going out to make a difference in the world."

Dorothy funded her scholarship through three gift annuities totaling $166,000. When asked if she would encourage others to consider a gift annuity, her response was immediate: "I don't think there could be a better investment. The returns from my annuities have been highly satisfactory. Knowing my financial gifts are being used in God's work is important to me and is very rewarding."

> **What leads to great gifts is a passion for your institution's mission.**

During the seminary's capital campaign, several other faculty and staff also made six-figure gifts. What can we learn from these happy surprises? Great wealth does not necessarily lead to great gifts. What leads to great gifts is a passion for your institution's mission. Look to those who know you best and who share your institution's values. In those people you will undoubtedly find some happy surprises!

Notes

12

The First Gift Is Often Just the Beginning

Beth made her first gift to the seminary in honor of her pastor. The pastor was celebrating sixty years in ministry, and the church honored him by establishing a scholarship in his name at his alma mater. Members of the congregation were invited to contribute.

Beth had heard of our seminary, but she'd had no personal interactions with it. "I certainly wanted to support the scholarship," she said, "but I didn't know enough about the seminary." So, she did her homework. She talked to a pastor friend who had gone to the seminary years earlier, as well as a recent graduate, about the seminary's reputation. Both assured her that a gift to the seminary would be a good investment.

She decided the seminary was a place worthy of her support. "I might not agree with every single thing the seminary does, but it was pretty close to a perfect fit," she noted. And so she made her first gift of $1,000 to the scholarship honoring her pastor.

I visited her soon thereafter to thank her for her support. I shared our campaign booklet with her, focusing especially on the page about endowed scholarships. I told her that her gift was helping us address one of our most important challenges—providing much-needed financial aid to deserving students. Beth was engaged throughout my presentation, asking good questions as we went along. It was a delightful visit.

A month later, I received a phone call from Beth. She said she had appreciated learning more about the seminary and our campaign during our recent visit. Her new knowledge got her thinking that perhaps the seminary would be a worthy place to invest more of her resources to ensure the training of strong Christian leaders. She wanted me to know that she would be talking to her financial advisor and would be back in touch when she knew what she was able to do.

Beth called again two months later. She had just received our gift annuity mailing and had a number of questions about how gift annuities work. She was very pleased to learn that she could get a better return than she was getting on her certificates of deposit, much of it tax-free, along with a nice charitable deduction—and that she would be doing good at the same time by helping train future church leaders.

Shortly thereafter, Beth took out a $70,000 gift annuity to start a scholarship in her own name. This was followed by four more annuities over the next few years to bring her total giving to more than $100,000—a wonderful legacy that started with a gift of $1,000.

What can we learn from this happy surprise? The first gift is often just the beginning—especially if the donor is thanked promptly and personally and is informed about the good the gift is doing.

Notes

Never Underestimate What Donors Can Do

13

As a part of our seminary's 150th anniversary capital campaign, we identified 150 areas where we hoped to host small informational gatherings. These events were hosted by key seminary friends at their homes, churches, or country clubs, often around a meal or dessert. The events were designed to introduce new potential friends to the seminary and its campaign, to answer any questions guests may have, and hopefully to inspire them to become involved in supporting our campaign goals.

And so, one spring day, I drove four and a half hours to a community in Iowa to tell the seminary's story to a gathering hosted by one of our trustees. The average size for these events was usually between twenty and twenty-five people, most of them people who knew little or nothing about the seminary. I was hoping this event would be similar.

Thus, I was surprised, and disappointed, when I walked in to discover there were only twelve present—including me! I was further disappointed when I looked around the room and realized there wasn't a new face in the group. Instead, they were all alums who, while supportive, were not considered to be major donor prospects. *Oh dear,* I thought. *These folks already know about the seminary and the campaign, and there's very little potential here.* Nonetheless, I made the presentation, answered a few questions, and then packed up my materials as I prepared to make the four-and-a-half-hour trek home.

That's when an older couple approached me. "Thank you," they said. "That was very informative. You've given us something to think about. We will be in touch."

A few weeks later a woman named Juanita called to say that after the event they had gone home and talked and prayed about what they had learned—and they had an idea. Years earlier, she had inherited a farm as a gift. Perhaps it was time to gift it again. Since her family had been deeply involved in the church and since her husband was so appreciative of his seminary training, they decided the best gift they could give would be to provide scholarships for ministerial students, thereby helping to address the need for well-trained pastors.

They gifted the farm and created a charitable remainder annuity trust from the proceeds. During their lifetimes they will receive income from the trust. Following their deaths, the remainder interest will go to Garrett-Evangelical to provide scholarships for those preparing for pastoral ministry.

Be open to surprises, because they are simply that—unexpected.

Juanita said they would also tithe to the seminary the income they receive from the trust so the seminary could begin awarding scholarships right away and they could experience the joy of knowing some of the people they are helping to train.

Juanita summarized their feelings with these words: "The farm was a gift to me, and I am grateful to give it back. Our prayers are that this gift will bless many lives in future years." And so it has!

What can we learn from this happy surprise? Never underestimate what donors can do. Some of the happiest surprises come when and where we least expect them!

Notes

14

No Response Does Not Mean No Interest

Tom also attended a small informational gathering hosted by a member of his church. He seemed to enjoy the occasion and said he appreciated learning more about the seminary's 150th anniversary campaign. Even though he lived close to the seminary and was active in a nearby congregation, he had not been on campus.

Following the event, I sought to contact Tom for a follow-up visit, as I did with everyone who attended a small informational gathering. The purpose of these visits was to receive their feedback, to answer any questions they may have, and to explore with them how they might like to be involved in our campaign.

I called Tom on the phone but always got his voicemail. After leaving numerous voicemail messages over a period of several weeks—and receiving no response—I finally decided that Tom must not have been as interested as he appeared to be at the gathering.

Eventually I resorted to sending him a follow-up letter inviting him to call me if he had any feedback he wanted to share or any questions he wanted answered. I also enclosed a gift intention form for him to fill out and return if he wanted to participate in our campaign. I concluded the letter by saying, "I hope to hear from you in the days ahead," although, in reality, I had very little hope that I would hear back from him.

It was therefore a very happy surprise when a few weeks later Tom returned the gift intention form, along with a check for $12,500 with "150th campaign" written in the memo line.

So, he was interested after all! We thanked him immediately, of course, and hoped he would be interested in continuing the conversation. However, it took nearly two more years before he agreed to visit the campus. After touring the campus and receiving an update on our campaign, he indicated he was prepared to make an additional $25,000 commitment.

Tom continued to give at that level for the next few years, as well as an additional gift for the annual fund, until we convinced him it was time to visit the campus again. In addition to thanking him for his contin-

> Sometimes "No" does not mean "Never." It just might mean "Not now."

ued support and updating him on our now-increased campaign goal, we explored with him the possibility of joining our board of trustees. He said he would be very interested in contributing to Garrett-Evangelical in a new way. Another happy surprise!

After joining the board, Tom made another multiyear commitment to the campaign, increased his annual fund support, included the seminary in his estate plans, and provided outstanding leadership as a trustee.

What can we learn from these happy surprises? "No response" does not mean "No interest." A corollary to Tom's story is that "No" does not necessarily mean "Never." It just might mean "Not now."

Notes

Expand Your Friendship Base

Current Friends Are the Best Source for New Friends

15

One day Myrta called me to say she had invited Wes to join the two of us for lunch. Myrta was a seminary trustee, and she took seriously her responsibility to introduce others to the seminary. Wes and Myrta both lived in a retirement community. Wes's late wife and Myrta had been close friends and active members of the same church.

Wes was no stranger to the church either. Born in a parsonage, Wes liked to comment that there was always plenty of "God talk" around when he was growing up. With a wry sense of humor, he would tell folks that his father, a minister, was in the fire insurance business.

Wes discovered his calling in architecture, and he spent the majority of his career designing schools and office buildings. However, the church, where both he and his wife sang in the choir, was their focal point.

Despite growing up in the parsonage and being active in the church all his life, Wes had not given a lot of thought to how or where ministers were trained—until the day of the lunch. Over lunch Myrta invited me to share with Wes a bit about the seminary, the cost of theological education, and the financial challenges that most seminary students face in order to pursue their call to ministry.

Then Myrta shared with Wes the joy she had experienced in creating a scholarship at the seminary and getting to meet the scholarship recipients. Next, she looked him straight in the eye and said, "Wes, you should consider doing something similar." A seed was planted.

Wes did not immediately respond, but two years later he made his first gift to the seminary—a memorial gift to Myrta's scholarship when she passed away. Two years later Wes indicated he wanted to do something in memory of his parents. He decided to honor their years of ministry by establishing a scholarship in their names with an initial gift of $44,000.

Friends can introduce new friends to your organization.

He added to it each year until it grew to more than $115,000. He, too, experienced the joy of meeting his scholarship recipients.

When Wes passed away, the seminary learned it was a beneficiary of his estate and would receive a bequest in excess of $750,000 for the scholarship he had started in memory of his parents. I am forever grateful to Wes for his generosity—and to Myrta for inviting him to lunch!

What can we learn from this happy surprise? Current friends are the best source for new friends. They know others who share their interests and values. Encourage them to introduce their friends to your organization.

Notes

16

Pastors Can Be Door Openers

Pastors can also open the door to potential new friends, as the following happy surprise illustrates. Bob and Shirley were introduced to the seminary many years ago when their pastor hosted a small informational gathering for some key members of the church. Bob and Shirley were pillars in the congrega-

Pastors can open doors that might otherwise be closed to your organization.

tion. Shirley provided leadership for a senior citizens group in the church, and Bob was a key member of the finance committee and served as church treasurer.

At the gathering, the pastor shared how grateful he was for his seminary education, before turning it over to me to tell the seminary's story. After that introductory meeting, in which they learned that many of their pastors had been trained at Garrett-Evangelical, Bob and Shirley began sending

60

an annual gift to the seminary to help train future church leaders. They also became members of our council of laity, an informal network of laypeople willing to serve as ambassadors for the seminary.

Bob retired after twenty-five years as a commodities broker. The following year he and Shirley visited the seminary for the first time and were able to tour the campus and meet some students and faculty. Shortly thereafter, they established an endowed scholarship in their names with a $50,000 gift. They delighted in meeting their scholarship recipient at the annual scholarship lunch each year that followed for a number of years.

During their early retirement years, Bob and Shirley spent half of each year in Florida and the other half in Illinois. Retirement life was not always easy, however. The company where Bob had worked for so many years went bankrupt, placing his pension funds in jeopardy. It took many years before the matter was settled in his favor.

One year was particularly challenging for them. The year began with Bob having gallbladder surgery. Later in the year Shirley was diagnosed with a brain tumor and underwent radiation and chemotherapy. While visiting her in the hospital, Bob had a heart attack and underwent quadruple bypass surgery.

Throughout all their personal and medical crises, however, they remained upbeat and never wavered in their interest in and support for the seminary. In fact, Bob would call me to apologize if their check was late because of a medical crisis. They continued to make a leadership gift to the seminary each year, in good times and bad.

Shirley lost her battle with cancer, and Bob suffered a blood clot on the brain that required surgery and months of rehabilitation. He decided to make Florida his permanent home. No longer able to attend the annual scholarship lunch, he relished my visits each winter. He would always inquire about his scholarship recipient and would proudly share the letters he received from that student.

During one such visit he shared with me that he had revised his estate plans and that Garrett-Evangelical would someday receive a substantial gift. While his health continued to decline over the next several years, his indomitable spirit did not.

Then one day, I received a phone call from the executors of Bob's estate, informing me that Bob had died and that Garrett-Evangelical would indeed receive a substantial gift. More than $2 million would be received for scholarship and unrestricted endowment support.

What can we learn from this happy surprise? Pastors know their people. They know who might share your organization's vision and who might have the ability to support it financially if properly informed and motivated. Enlist their support to help tell your story.

Notes

Volunteers Can Become Great Donors

17

"If you want something done right, just ask a busy person." That old adage proved true when I asked Chrys to help organize a small informational gathering as a part of our Forging Our Future campaign. Although she was already deeply involved in church and community activities, she was recommended by her pastor as someone who would do a great job in coordinating such an event.

"I'm a good organizer, and that's my problem," Chrys said. "I can't say no. I'm hard on myself. If I say I'll do it, then I'll do it 150 percent. I have a hard time relaxing, and I like to be busy."

So Chrys said yes to organizing the gathering—and it was a big success. In fact, she so impressed me with her leadership and organizational skills that we invited her to join the seminary's board of trustees. Again, she said yes, this time because of her deep commitment to the church and her recognition that preparing outstanding leaders for the church needed to be a high priority.

Years before, Chrys met her future husband in college. They married, raised two children, and became deeply involved in the life of the community. Chrys became a leader in the church, serving as trustee, stewardship chair, membership chair, vacation Bible school chair, pastor-parish relations chair, administrative council chair, revisioning committee chair, and fund for discipleship chair.

Those who share their time and their talent are likely to share their treasure.

Chrys's leadership didn't stop at the church. When her children were young, she started the citywide Parent-Teacher Organization. She worked on capital campaigns for the Girl Scouts and an art center. She was a founding member of an organization with a mission to empower the lives of women.

"I guess you could call me a proper activist," she noted. "I'm interested in creating social change, not just putting a Band-Aid on a problem. My full-time job was donating forty to fifty hours a week to organizations I care deeply about."

Why was such a busy layperson willing to give her precious time to a seminary, first to coordinate an event and later as a trustee? Chrys summarized it well: "After every board meeting I was overwhelmed as I felt the arms of grace wrap around me. I got to break bread, pray, worship, and analyze important issues with a most incredible group of dedicated people moved by God to bring their own unique gifts to the table. I felt I received far more from this association than I could ever give back."

But give back she did, in generous measure, her time, her talent, and her treasure. She assumed a leadership role by chairing the student affairs committee of the board. She also assumed a leadership role in the seminary's Forging Our

Future campaign by establishing a scholarship in her name. This endowed scholarship, which is being funded with outright gifts and a planned gift commitment, will someday surpass $400,000, providing a leadership scholarship each year to an outstanding woman preparing for ministry.

What can we learn from this happy surprise? Those who are invited to share their time and their talent are also likely to share their treasure. Our task is to find ways to meaningfully involve others in the work of our organization.

Notes

18

Do You See a Pattern Here?

Yes, I was given Dan's name by his pastor also. Are you beginning to see a pattern here? I hope so! Dan's pastor suggested Dan would be a good coordinator for a celebration the seminary was planning in the pastor's honor. When I called to make an appointment, Dan volunteered to come to my office, as he wanted to see the campus anyway. On the day of the visit, I gave him a brief tour of the campus, ending up in my office to get acquainted. I shared with him our plans to honor his pastor and invited his assistance in planning the day. Dan was enthusiastic about our plans and thought it would be a fine way to affirm his pastor's ministry. He agreed to work with me to coordinate the event.

Dan did a wonderful job of coordinating the celebration in honor of his pastor, including making a $5,000 gift to the seminary to help establish a scholarship in his pastor's name.

I kept in touch with Dan following the event. He indicated a willingness to continue his leadership support to the scholarship he had helped establish. He visited campus several more times to do research in our library and to continue our conversations.

Dan struck me as a thoughtful, scholarly person who was deeply committed to the church. I asked him one day whether he would be interested in serv-ing on our board of trustees. He said he was flattered to be considered and would give it further thought.

He thought about it for a year, and then said he was open to being considered.

> There are many ways to involve volunteers in the work of your organization.

He also wanted me to know he had included the seminary in his will.

I wrote and thanked Dan for this wonderful news and asked him if he would be willing to fill out and return a mem-orandum of intention form sharing further details about his planned gift commitment. Shortly thereafter, Dan sent the form back. He indicated that, while the exact amount would not be known until the estate is finally settled, he believed a conservative estimate for his planned gift commitment would be $1 million!

What can we learn from this happy surprise? There are numerous ways to involve volunteers in the work of your orga-nization: hosting small informational gatherings, coordinating ministry Sundays, serving on a council of laity, becoming a trustee. Finding ways to meaningfully involve people in volun-teer activities is a wonderful way to give them an insider's view of your organization—and a wonderful way to deepen their commitment of your organization.

Notes

Encourage Intergenerational Giving

19

Another wonderful way to expand your friendship base is to encourage intergenerational giving, just as Joan did. Joan was pleased when two of her father's former associate pastors decided to honor him by inviting friends and parishioners to contribute to an endowed scholarship fund in his name at our seminary, her father's alma mater. She was proud of her father and his years of ministry, and she knew he had positively touched the lives of many people.

Joan also knew that her father appreciated his seminary training, and she was deeply touched to learn that her parents were also contributing to the scholarship. "My father never wanted to call attention to himself," she said, "but when he realized that this scholarship could help train other pastors, he thought it was a wonderful thing to support."

Joan decided she should do the same. She made a gift of $5,000 to the scholarship. When I visited her to thank her for her fine support, she wanted to know how much scholarship assistance was generated each year. When I told her how much was available to be awarded each year and how much it costs a student each year to attend seminary, she realized that the scholarship didn't begin to cover the total cost. Joan indicated she would be open to adding to the scholarship, and I encouraged her to consider doing so on an annual basis.

Joan did continue to add to the scholarship, and one year she was able to come to campus and have lunch with the scholarship recipient. That really sparked her interest in the scholarship. She began writing the scholarship recipients and encouraging them in their studies. And she continued to add to the scholarship each year—gifts of $1,000, $5,000, $10,000, and even $100,000—helping it grow to more than $300,000. She also shared that she has remembered this scholarship with a significant gift in her estate plan. But Joan did not stop there. She said she feels so strongly about this scholarship that she has asked her four daughters to skip presents on her birthday and Christmas and give to the scholarship instead. The strategy has worked, and her daughters have begun to contribute to the scholarship as well.

Joan sees this scholarship as a way to keep her parents' legacy alive. Her hope is that her daughters will help carry on the legacy for years to come. "My parents had a huge impact on my daughters," she said. "I know this scholarship is important to them." Giving back and being a role model are important to Joan. "I hope that my generation can leave our small part of the world better than we found it and set an example for our children and grandchildren to do the same," she said.

What can we learn from this happy surprise? This is a great example of how several generations can get involved with an organization. Joan's parents supported the seminary, Joan supports it, and now her daughters support it. Organizations that encourage intergenerational giving can also experience happy surprises like this.

Notes

Find Ways to Honor Others

Honor Your Father and Mother

20

We have learned that, just as church members are open to honoring their pastor, children are often open to honoring their parents. Sally is a good example. Sally received a large financial settlement as the result of a serious accident. While most of the money was reserved for her care, she also wanted to use some of the proceeds to support organizations she cared deeply about. Although she was not personally familiar with our seminary, she knew how much her father appreciated his seminary education. And so, she contacted us to explore the possibility of making a gift in his honor.

Sally was delighted to learn that one of the seminary's biggest challenges was providing financial assistance to deserving students and that she could create an endowed scholarship to do that. She immediately agreed to do so. Shortly thereafter, the seminary received a check for $50,000 to create an endowed scholarship in honor of her father. Needless to say, he was moved to tears when he learned what she had done.

That was the beginning of a wonderful relationship. Sally and her father both enjoyed hearing from the scholarship recipients each year, and they were even able to visit the campus and meet several of their recipients over the years.

Sally later added her mother's name to the scholarship since she was truly a partner in ministry with her father. When her father died, he remembered the scholarship in his estate plans.

Sally has continued to add to the scholarship each year for the past thirty-five years. She has also earmarked matching gift funds from her former employer for the scholarship. It has now grown to $350,000 and is one of the seminary's premier scholarships.

Children are often looking for ways to honor their parents, ways that reflect their values and create a legacy.

As her knowledge of the seminary grew, so did her interest. In addition to supporting the scholarship, Sally became a regular contributor to the annual fund and made commitments to other seminary goals as well, including faculty support, unrestricted endowment, and improving campus facilities.

What can we learn from this happy surprise? Children are often looking for meaningful ways to honor their parents, ways that reflect their values and create a legacy in their names. Organizations that are near and dear to parents can also become near and dear to their children with proper cultivation, invitation, and stewardship.

Notes

Honor Your Spouse

21

We have also learned that a spouse is often moved to honor his or her beloved mate through giving, either during their lifetimes or at the time of death.

Shirley is a good example of the former. One day she called me on the phone to say she wanted to surprise her husband, an alum of our seminary, by starting a scholarship in his name. She wanted to know how much it would cost to endow a scholarship and what was required to get one established. She told me how proud she was of his ministry and her hope to inform him of this scholarship when the family was gathered together for an Easter celebration.

I told her that her phone call was an answer to prayer, since one of the biggest challenges at the seminary was providing adequate scholarship assistance to deserving students. I said we were proud to claim him as an alum and would be delighted to have his name permanently affiliated with the seminary through such a scholarship.

Shirley concluded the call by saying she would put a check in the mail for $25,000 that day and looked forward to working with me to continue growing the scholarship in the future. She would continue to add to the scholarship, she said, and hoped that others would want to add to it as well.

Shirley later sent names of others (family members, friends, and professional colleagues) who she thought would be interested in learning about this scholarship. A letter was sent to these folks from the seminary, informing them of this newly formed scholarship and inviting them to add to it if they wished. A press release was also sent out, and a number of additional gifts were received.

Shirley continues to add to the scholarship each year and has also included the seminary in her estate plans, ensuring that the scholarship will ultimately exceed $100,000!

Avis started a scholarship in memory of her husband, also an alum, on the first anniversary of his death, as a lasting tribute to his years of ministry and as a way to make it possible for others to follow in his footsteps. She too made an initial gift of $25,000 and has continued to make significant gifts each year since, ensuring that it will also exceed $100,000.

What can we learn from Shirley and Avis? Spouses are often eager to carry on the values of their mates and create a lasting legacy in their names. Organizations that recognize this and can find meaningful ways to create such legacies will also open the door to many happy surprises!

Notes

Honor Your Children

22

Inara turned a terrible tragedy into a living memorial. Her two daughters were killed in a car accident on their way to visit their only grandparent for Grandparents Day, just two weeks before one of the daughters was to start seminary.

Inara's church was there for her during this most difficult time. "I cannot imagine what I would have done without my church," she said. "It gave me so much support." She also attended a support group for grieving parents. There she observed that those with a church affiliation seemed to cope far better.

A few months after this tragic event, Inara called to say she wanted to visit the seminary and have a conversation about honoring the memory of her daughters. On the day of the visit, she spoke openly about the support she had received from her church, from friends, and even from strangers. She then shared her desire to endow a scholarship at the seminary in memory of her one daughter and at a college for her other daughter. She was eager to work out the details for how this could be put in place.

"It was very important to me to establish this scholarship at the seminary," she said. "I wanted to help carry on through others what my daughter had hoped to do. I think that can best be accomplished by supporting the education and the goals of individuals with aspirations that are similar to my daughter's."

Inara established the scholarship with an initial gift of $5,000—and continues to add to it each year with generous gifts so that it has grown to more than $250,000. "Establishing the scholarship through outright gifts has enabled me to see the use of my funds during my lifetime and to see the fruits of my decision. I treasure the notes from the recipients of the scholarship. Their notes express the importance of financial support in their quest toward a degree."

Inara has also included the seminary in her estate plans. "After my death, even more students will be able to receive assistance from the scholarship through my will commitment. It gives me great satisfaction to know that this scholarship in my daughter's name will live on in perpetuity."

What can we learn from Inara? Hers is a story of an individual overcoming tragedy, drawing upon a solid spiritual center, and forming a strong connection to the seminary. Organizations that stand with people during times of tragedy as well as triumph will create lifelong friends—and yes, even happy surprises.

Notes

People Want to
Leave a Legacy

How Much Does It Cost to Create a Scholarship?

23

One day I received a phone call from Christabel. She had made a small gift a year earlier to a scholarship in honor of her pastor. She had become acquainted with the seminary through that scholarship and, subsequently, through the seminary's quarterly magazine that she had begun receiving after making her gift.

She called me to say she was considering another gift to the seminary. "Wonderful!" I said. "Would you like to designate it toward the scholarship in honor of your pastor once again?"

"Well, actually, I was considering a scholarship in my own name," she replied. "Would you be able to come and visit me and help me understand how to do that?" "Of course," I answered. A few days later I was sitting in her living room, where she showed me her seminary file folder containing every piece of literature she had received from the seminary since making her first gift.

"How much does it cost to create a scholarship?" she asked. "The minimum goal for an endowed scholarship is $25,000," I responded. Before I could say "and that can be built over a period of time," she said, "Oh, I can write you a check for that amount today." She went on to say, "I can probably do the same thing next year."

Then she told me her life story. She had always wanted to be a teacher, but her parents couldn't afford to send her to college. That's when Christabel's pastor stepped in. He wanted to help her go to college and was able to secure a scholarship for her. She was able to graduate from college and fulfill her life's dream of being an elementary school teacher.

Christabel was forever grateful for her pastor's assistance. Therefore, she decided she wanted to help train other pastors like him by creating a scholarship at the seminary. "Because of the help I got through my church, I thought, at age eighty-eight, that I would like to help a good student earn an advanced degree from the seminary," she stated.

Gifts of kindness and support can have a ripple effect over many years.

She was delighted to come to campus and meet her first scholarship recipient and to become an "angel" to students who—like her—could not pursue their dreams without scholarship assistance.

Following her visit to the campus, she shared with me that she planned to include the seminary in her estate planning. She had no children of her own, so this was a way she could leave a legacy. When she passed away a few years later, Garrett-Evangelical was the major beneficiary of her estate, receiving more than $725,000 to be added to her scholarship!

What can we learn from this happy surprise? Christabel's story reminds us that gifts of kindness and support can have a ripple effect over many years. Her pastor's support touched not only her life but the lives of many others that Christabel positively influenced through her years of teaching. Likewise, Christabel's scholarship will enrich not only students' lives but also the communities that will be touched by their ministries. Her legacy lives on!

Notes

24

We've Changed Our Minds

Jerry checked the box on our business reply envelope that read: "I have provided for the seminary in my will/trust." As an alum, he had been a regular contributor to the seminary's annual fund, but this was the first we knew of his planned gift commitment. I wrote him immediately to thank him for sharing this information with us and to invite him to share more details of his plans if he was willing to do so.

Jerry filled out a memorandum of intention form, indicating that he was designating one-sixth of his estate to the seminary. What a happy surprise!

The following year, Jerry and his wife, Holly, attended a small informational gathering at their church and learned about the seminary's capital campaign. At the conclusion of the event, they encouraged me to keep in touch. And so, I made a point of visiting them the next time I was in the area.

We had a pleasant two-hour visit. Jerry told me about his career as a minister, and Holly told me about her career as a professor of education. They also asked a number of good questions about the seminary's campaign goals.

Then came a surprise. "We've changed our minds," they said. They informed me that the planned giving figure they had shared with me earlier was no longer accurate. Originally their plan was to divide their estate

> It is up to us to steward people with planned gift commitments to keep their passion alive.

six ways, and we were to receive one-sixth. However, after attending the small informational gathering and learning about the seminary's long-term goals, they revised their wills. They wanted me to know that the seminary would now receive five-sixths of their estate. Furthermore, they thought their estate would probably continue to grow, as they have invested wisely and live relatively simply.

Jerry asked me to send him a new memorandum of intention form to fill out. I told him I could do better than that—and reached into my folder and handed him one. They decided they would fill it out right then and there—an unrestricted planned gift commitment for $1 million!

What can we learn from this happy surprise? Most planned gift commitments are not set in stone. They can decrease or increase in value depending on investments and, even more important, a donor's passion for an organization's mission. It is up to us to steward people with planned gift commitments to keep that passion alive!

Notes

25

Would You Like Some Farmland?

Bob grew up in rural Kansas. Marilyn grew up in rural Illinois. They met at a social for new students during their first week at seminary. A year later they were married. When they graduated, they moved to Bob's home state, where they served churches for several years. Then Bob was invited to work for a national church organization in New York. They served in New York for the next twenty-five years.

They never forgot their Midwestern roots, however, or their deep appreciation for their seminary education. They were faithful leadership donors to the seminary, helping to start an endowed scholarship for Kansas students and helping to create an endowed chair for a beloved faculty member. And when they retired, they moved back to Illinois.

When the seminary launched its Endowing for Excellence campaign in the 1980s, they informed us that the seminary was a beneficiary in their trust. "Would you like some farmland someday?" they asked. A happy surprise!

When the seminary was preparing to launch its Forging Our Future campaign in 2002, I visited them and invited them to be honorary cochairs of the campaign. They agreed to serve in this capacity and to help set the pace for the campaign. They then shared with me that they had recently revised their trust and that Garrett-Evangelical would now receive more of the trust assets. Another happy surprise!

When the campaign goal was raised to $100 million in 2010, Bob and Marilyn again updated their estate plans. They indicated that land values had increased and therefore their planned gift commitment had increased as well. Another happy surprise!

> **Some of our best past donors can be some of our best future donors.**

In 2017 they contacted me for some assistance in planned giving. They were redoing their trusts once again and wanted some help with the language. In 2018 they invited me to join them for a meal at their condo. They shared with me that they had finally received copies of their revised trusts, and they wanted me to know they had gifted even more land to the seminary. I left a memorandum of intention form with them and encouraged them to fill it out with a revised estimate of their total planned gift commitment so we could count their additional commitment toward a future campaign.

Marilyn called me a few days later to say that they were filling out the memorandum of intention form, and she wanted me to know what the revised estimate for their planned gift commitment would be. I could hardly believe what I was hearing, so I asked her to clarify. She said we would be receiving some Illinois farmland, some Kansas farmland, and some other assets, for a grand total of several million dollars. I thanked her profusely for this outstanding commitment. A very happy surprise!

What can we learn from all these happy surprises? Some of our best past donors are more than likely some of our best future donors, especially if we have continued to inform them and meaningfully involve them in the work of our organization. Don't assume that past major donors can't do more.

Notes

Other Important Learnings

Unhappy Surprises Can Become Happy Surprises

26

Charles was a leadership donor. He also had included the seminary in his estate plans with a nice planned gift commitment. I called him one day to arrange a stewardship visit to thank him for his support and to bring him up to date on the seminary.

"You can come for a visit if you want," Charles said, "but you need to know I have taken the seminary out of my will." He went on to say that he planned to end his monthly giving as well because of what he perceived to be the seminary's overemphasis on issues he did not consider important.

As I was trying to decide if I wanted to drive an hour to his home to have him repeat what he had just told me on the phone, an idea popped into my head. "Why don't you come to campus and have lunch with the president and me so you can share your concerns directly with her," I suggested. After a long pause he finally responded, "Well, I suppose I could do so."

Next, I had to invite the president to have lunch with a disgruntled donor. "This may be a waste of your time," I confessed. Nonetheless, she immediately agreed to the lunch, and on the day of the meeting, she stood outside to personally welcome Charles and hand him his parking pass.

Charles and the president had a chance to get acquainted during lunch, and he shared with us some of his frustrations with other organizations with which he was involved. Then I invited Charles to share his concerns about the seminary. The president listened with empathy and compassion and then helped put these issues in a broader context by sharing elements from the seminary's recently adopted strategic plan. She thanked Charles for sharing his concerns and said that she needed to hear them, as it would help her provide a more balanced articulation of the seminary's vision going forward.

Charles, in turn, thanked her for listening so well and responding so well to his concerns. He said he has not had that experience when he has tried to share his concerns with other organizations, and thus he no longer supports them.

When people feel their concerns are heard, they are more open to listening.

The president needed to leave for another appointment, but Charles and I continued the conversation for a while. As we walked back to my office, I encouraged him to reconsider his decision to remove the seminary from his will. "Oh, I already have," he said. "Do you have a memorandum of intention form for me to fill out?" I assured him I did!

As Charles filled out the form back in my office, I hoped that he wouldn't reduce his $100,000 planned gift commitment. When he handed me the form, I saw it was not for $100,000. He indicated the seminary would now be in his will for $150,000! He said he would continue his monthly giving as well.

What can we learn from this happy surprise? This visit was a powerful reminder that when people feel their concerns have been heard, their anger and frustration often diminish or even disappear. I told the president I was going to find some more disgruntled donors and invite them to join her for lunch!

Notes

27 Timing Is Everything

James was invited to a small informational gathering in Florida in March. The hosts invited everyone from their church who they knew had a summer home in the Midwest. (The church directory helpfully provided that information.)

James responded that he could not attend the gathering but that he would be interested in visiting the seminary when he returned to his home in Illinois. I called him throughout the summer, and finally in late October he agreed to visit campus. Since he was ninety years old and no longer drove, I drove to his home some forty-five minutes away and picked him up. We attended a chapel service, had lunch in the cafeteria, took a campus tour, and ended up in my office, where I shared with him what he would have heard had he been able to attend the small informational gathering.

At the end of the presentation, James indicated that he would like to do something for the seminary. When I asked him what level of gift he was considering, he said he wanted to give that further thought. I drove him back home, which provided a wonderful opportunity to learn more about his career, his family, and his current interests.

In November I received a phone call from James saying that he was transferring $37,657 worth of stock to establish a scholarship in memory of his wife. We kept in touch over the months, and six months later I received another phone call from James saying he was once again transferring

> **When there are people to listen, we must be ready to tell the story of our organization.**

stock—this time worth $43,737. He said his goal was to bring the scholarship to the $100,000 level—a goal he accomplished by the time he died at age ninety-eight.

What can we learn from James and this happy surprise? Several things: first, timing is everything. James shared with me that shortly before receiving our invitation to the gathering in Florida, he had begun to do some estate planning. Because the church was important to him, he was thinking about leaving something to a church-related organization. Our invitation arrived at the right time.

Second, there are people in each of our neighborhoods who are very receptive to hearing more about our organizations, and we need to be equally open to telling our story time and time again whenever and wherever we can.

Finally, some of our best prospects may well be those who are invited to attend a gathering but, for whatever reason, don't attend. Thus, we need to make sure we follow up not only with those who attend our gatherings but also with those who do not attend but who express a willingness to learn more. If the timing isn't right on the first try, maybe it will be on the second or third attempt.

Notes

Never Judge a Book by Its Cover

28

A seminary colleague gave me the name of someone that his friend told him I might want to meet. "I'm not sure why you'd want to meet him, though, because he was at the same meeting my friend and I were at. By the way he dressed, I don't think he has a penny to his name."

I accepted the challenge, nonetheless, and wrote down his name. The next time I was in Indianapolis, I made it a point to meet Russ. His clothes were indeed old and worn. Beneath his appearance, however, I discovered a very savvy business-man, and we had an enjoyable two-hour visit. I learned that he was ninety years old, that he had graduated with a bachelor's degree in architectural engineering, and that he had worked as a construction engineer for several years before becoming co-owner of a construction firm. I also learned that he had grown up on a farm, which he later inherited. He still owned the land, though it was no longer a farm but a large commercial development that leased the land from him, thereby providing him with a very nice income.

Finally, I learned that he had been a member of his local church for eighty-one years, serving as lay leader for more than twenty years. He commented that he was interested in anything related to the church. Thus, he was interested in learning more about the seminary and its capital campaign. I walked him through our campaign booklet and indicated our desire to involve committed church folks like him in our mission.

Russ expressed an interest in getting involved. He was particularly pleased that one of the seminary's key campaign goals was to attract an outstanding student body. He noted that over the years he had been the recipient of some very good pastors and also some very poor pastors, and he wanted to play a role in making sure there were more of the former and fewer of the latter.

Having established a scholarship at his own alma mater, he recognized the importance of leadership scholarships in attracting those students with the greatest potential for effective ministry. He also recognized it was important for church people like him to support theological education because, unlike many educational institutions, seminaries cannot depend solely on their alums to provide the scholarship assistance needed. He agreed to reflect further on what he personally might be interested in doing.

Sometimes happy surprises come from those you least expect can help you.

I visited Russ several more times over the next year. Each time he expressed an interest in doing something but indicated he was still reflecting on what he could do. On the anniversary of our first visit, he indicated his intention to give $5,000 a year for five years to establish a scholarship in his name. Unfortunately, he died a few months later. He had completed only one payment of his five-year commitment.

A few days after his death, however, I was notified that Russ had included the seminary in his will for a gift of $300,000—enough to permanently endow a leadership scholarship in his name.

What can we learn from this happy surprise? Never judge a book by its cover. Sometimes the happy surprises come from those individuals you least expect can help you.

Notes

Nothing Beats an On-Site Visit

29

For many years we have hosted a reunion for our fifty-year graduates. It is a special time when graduates can reconnect with classmates as well as experience what the seminary is like today. Many alums say they come back expecting that the seminary won't be as good as when they attended, but they leave their reunion convinced that the seminary is better than ever.

David was an alum who came back for his reunion a few years ago. He had not returned to the seminary since his graduation fifty years earlier. He participated in all the reunion activities, including a panel discussion with graduating seniors, a chapel service led by the graduating class, a special dinner with trustees and old friends, and the commencement service, where the fifty-year graduates were recognized.

David also heard a presentation about our Forging Our Future campaign and learned more about the seminary's long-term goals. When he returned home, he told his friends that he was so moved by his experience and so impressed with the seminary and its strategic vision for the future that he had decided to remember the seminary in his will.

After graduating from seminary years before, David went on to earn a PhD. He had served as a church pastor for several years before accepting the position of professor of religion at a small church-related college, where he served with distinction until his retirement.

Two years after his seminary reunion, David passed away. Shortly thereafter, with surprise and gratitude, the seminary learned that David had designated a $500,000 unrestricted bequest to the seminary. He had named his friends as coexecutors of his estate, and they worked gladly and carefully to fulfill his wishes because they remembered his enthusiasm upon his return from his fiftieth reunion. They also gave the seminary David's extensive library.

> **Nothing beats an on-site visit to meet the people, catch the vision, and experience the spirit of the place.**

What can we learn from this happy surprise? If at all possible, have alums, friends, and potential donors experience firsthand your organization's mission. Nothing beats an on-site visit where they can meet the people, catch the vision, and experience the spirit of the place.

Notes

30

People Will Stretch If Motivated

Phyllis had worked at the seminary for several years as an administrative assistant. When she retired, she moved to Florida with her husband. Over the years they were modest givers, never at the leadership level. Nevertheless, she remained interested in the seminary and read everything we sent her.

Thus, when she received an invitation to attend a small informational gathering near her home (in February, of course), she immediately responded that she and her husband would attend.

They seemed to enjoy themselves at the gathering. As the guests left, Phyllis approached me and said that she had written a check for $500 before coming to the gathering, which she had planned to give to me. However, after learning about our campaign, she had decided to go home and discuss with her husband if they could do more. She said I would be hearing from her in a few days.

A few days later, I did indeed receive a phone call from her. Phyllis said they had decided to increase their gift tenfold—from

$500 to $5,000! This was a significant gift for them—and they both felt very good about being able to make it.

What can we learn from this happy surprise? If people are properly informed and inspired, they will often stretch to do more than they had originally planned. Their gift, while not large by some standards, was a major gift for them. Their gift is also a good reminder that every gift, no matter what the size, is important in helping an organization reach its goals, and should be gratefully received and acknowledged.

All gifts are important in helping the organization reach its goals.

Notes

Putting It All Together

Stewardship Is Key

31

What inspires a layperson in Iowa to support a seminary in Illinois for more than thirty years? According to Joe, perhaps it was God speaking to him through a couple of individuals—and his faithful stewardship over the years.

Joe still remembers the day years ago when he got a phone call from his friend Bob, inviting him to a 7:30 a.m. breakfast to meet a young man from a seminary in Illinois. "I can't," Joe replied. "I'm at work then." "Call them and tell them you will be late!" Bob countered. So that is what Joe did—and the rest, as they say, is history!

Bob and Joe were both active church members, and both shared a deep appreciation for their pastor, a graduate of our seminary. Bob had been introduced to the seminary a couple of years earlier and was working with me to create an endowed scholarship in honor of their pastor. Bob thought Joe would be interested in learning more about the seminary and the plans to honor their pastor. Hence, the breakfast meeting.

At the breakfast, Joe shared with Bob and me his story of growing up on a farm, majoring in business administration in college, spending two years in the army, and then moving to Iowa to begin work at Rockwell Collins, where he worked his way up in management. Joe listened with interest as I told him about the seminary and how it had been preparing Christian leaders like his pastor since its founding in 1853.

Joe commented that he recognized the importance of higher education. Since he was a bachelor and had never sent anyone to college, he was thinking that perhaps he should help someone through school. Upon learning about the financial challenges seminarians face in funding three years of graduate theological education, he became convinced this was where he could make an important difference. At the conclusion of the visit, Joe remarked that perhaps God was speaking to him through Bob and me.

Shortly thereafter, Joe made a leadership gift to the scholarship in honor of his pastor—and he has continued his leadership support to the seminary every year since. He does so because he believes in the seminary's mission—and because he is visited every year, thanked for his gift, and brought up to date on the seminary.

First time donors can become annual donors.

In addition to his annual leadership gifts, Joe has made a significant planned gift commitment to the seminary through his will. "My hope is that these gifts will help make it possible for young people to pursue their call to ministry," Joe says. "I want to help prepare quality leaders like my own pastor and other graduates I have known."

Just as Joe was introduced to the seminary by a friend, he in turn has hosted several small informational gatherings over the years to introduce others to the seminary. And so, the circle of friendship continues to widen.

What can we learn from this happy surprise? First-time donors can become annual donors if they are regularly and personally thanked for their gifts and if they are helped to understand how their gifts are making an important difference. In short, stewardship is key!

Notes

32

Filthy Lucre Can Be Redeemed

When Thomas attended his fiftieth reunion, he was inspired to take out a $2,500 gift annuity with the seminary. He continued to take out a small annuity every year after that. Then one day, I received a message saying he had called and was ready to take out another annuity. He asked me to call him that afternoon to discuss what he wanted to do.

When I called, he said he had to tell me a story before we talked about annuities. The condensed version follows. As a retired pastor, Thomas provided pastoral counseling to workers at a casino about thirty miles south of where he lives. The casino provided a conference room for him to meet with those he counseled. One day he was waiting outside the conference room for a counseling appointment. To pass the time he dug some change out of his pocket and dropped a couple of coins into the penny slot machine next to him.

To his astonishment, he won the jackpot—more than $2,378,000—the largest jackpot ever on that machine! He was told his odds of winning were one in 25 million! He was immediately surrounded by security guards who whisked him away to a plush hotel room for his safety. The casino then sent a limo to pick up his wife and have her join him for the night.

The casino told him he would receive $118,000-plus for the next nineteen years. He told them that at eighty-two years of age, he would not live that long, and he wanted a lump sum instead. Thomas told me he had recently received that lump sum—a check for $1,600,000. Since then he had been receiving fifteen to twenty calls a day from friends and relatives he never knew he had!

Thomas said that he and his wife didn't need this money, and they wanted to be good stewards by sharing it with family and charity. He said he wanted the first check to go to the seminary since he deeply appreciated the education he had received. He was thinking of a gift annuity of $50,000.

Then it was my turn to speak. I decided to have some fun with him, since he had such fun telling me his story. I told him the board of trustees had met the previous week and had approved a plan to celebrate the seminary's 160th anniversary by encouraging alums and friends to make an extra-mile gift in one of the following amounts: $160, $1,600, $16,000, $160,000, or $1,600,000. (This is all true.) I teased him by saying it seemed providential that one of our distinguished alums had just received a check for $1,600,000 and that if he wanted to write a check to the seminary for that amount, he could avoid taxes entirely.

> Sometimes gifts come with funny stories and good storytellers.

Thomas laughed and said he wasn't ready to do that, as he also wanted to remember some other charities and help put his grandchildren through college. He was open, however, to expanding his vision—and he ended up taking out another gift annuity for $90,000!

What can we learn from this happy surprise? No, it's not to play the penny slot machines! It's that gifts sometimes come with funny stories—and good storytellers! And that filthy lucre can be redeemed!

Notes

Remember to Pray

33

As we celebrated the seminary's first twenty-five years of leadership in spiritual formation studies, we recognized that it was uniquely positioned to continue enhancing studies in this area. However, this could only happen if there would continue to be a full-time faculty person teaching in spiritual formation. Thus, seminary administrators decided to raise $2 million to permanently endow a faculty position and to name it in honor of one of its distinguished alums, Bishop Rueben Job. Bishop Job had been at the forefront in spiritual formation within the life of the church, serving as a consultant in Christian spirituality, a spiritual retreat leader, a spiritual guide, and an author of more than twenty books.

A committee was formed, and the seminary publicly launched its fundraising efforts in April 2010. Hundreds of people responded out of deep appreciation for Bishop Job's ministry and in recognition of the importance of such an endowed faculty position at a seminary.

However, by October 2012, the seminary had raised less than half of what was needed to fully endow the chair. That month committee members had a conference call with Bishop Job to inform him of the status of the fundraising efforts and to let him know that the current professor would be retiring at the end of 2012. If the chair was not fully funded by then, the faculty position would have to remain vacant until the funds were raised.

"Are you sure you have done everything you can do?" Bishop Job asked. He had offered his name and endorsement to this endeavor, recognizing that this faculty position would continue his life's work when he was no longer alive. Now in frail health, would he live to see this dream fulfilled?

Following the conference call, committee members talked about what else we could do. We had made numerous personal visits, written countless letters, and hosted a number of gatherings. What more could we do?

That night it struck me that perhaps we had not done enough of the one thing Bishop Job emphasized throughout his ministry—pray! I began to pray each day that God would lead us to one or more individuals who could help complete the funding for this endowed chair.

A couple of weeks later, I received an email from someone I did not know. She introduced herself as Billie and said she was the lay leader of a small-membership church in rural Texas. She had taken a weekend class entitled "What God Wants for Your Life." It was there she first heard of spiritual direction and learned of a new two-year training program in spiritual direction being offered. She signed up for the program, and it had a profound impact on her spiritual journey.

"People in the pews need what seminaries offer," she wrote, "not just through the education of our pastors, but through access to those wonderful teaching resources ourselves!" She went on to say, "It is my understanding that your seminary has a commitment to spiritual formation through the work of the Rueben Job chair." She wrote me to say she wanted to know more.

I immediately called her, and we had an encouraging one-hour phone conversation. I learned that she and her husband were in the early stages of setting up a family foundation with $1 million. They were also interested in the possibility of making an initial gift of $250,000 before the end of the year to an organization that shared their vision and hopes. She was especially interested in strengthening the connection between rural churches and seminaries in the area of spiritual formation. Hence, her interest in learning more about the Rueben Job chair.

I explained that the goal for the chair was $2 million and thus far we had raised $750,000. I told her we were eager to fully fund the chair as soon as possible so we could move forward in hiring a professor to replace our retiring professor. I told her they could make that a reality if they wanted to give the full $1.25 million to the seminary instead of starting a family foundation. She said she didn't think they would be prepared to do that, as they wanted to create a family foundation.

> **Don't forget to call on God, your biggest advocate, when you pray.**

We agreed that this was just an exploratory conversation. I encouraged her to visit our website to learn more about the seminary and our spiritual formation program.

Billie called me the next day to say that she had spent most of the night reading about the Rueben Job chair on our website, praying about it, and discussing it with her husband. "We have decided the family foundation can wait," she said. "We would like to give $1.25 million to the seminary—before the end of the year—to fully fund the Rueben Job Chair in Spiritual Formation."

We had the joy of calling Bishop Job with this wonderful news. He in turn immediately wrote Billie to say, "It is difficult to describe how thrilled I was to learn about your wonderful gift to the Rueben Job Chair in Spiritual Formation. Your gift is indeed an answer to many prayers, including my own. . . . My prayers of petition have turned to prayers of thanksgiving, and you will be a part of those prayers as long as I live."

What can we learn from this happy surprise? God works in mysterious ways. Remember to pray!

Notes

Build Long-Term Relationships

34

I sometimes tell fundraisers that our job is to grow oak trees, not tomato plants. What I mean is this: We are not trying to grow something that lasts only a short period of time. Rather, we are seeking to grow something enduring. More specifically, we are seeking to build long-term relationships rather than seeking a quick gift.

> **Fundraisers grow oak trees, not tomato plants.**

When fundraisers focus on building long-term relationships, amazing things happen. We see donors in their fullness, with many different gifts, including perhaps the gift of financial resources. We see them as our partners, collaborating with us on projects that will give them, as well as us, great joy. We see them not just as donors, but as friends—friendships that are built on mutual trust and respect. And more often than not, it is when these long-term relationships are nurtured that happy surprises result.

Ernie is a good example. You met Ernie earlier, where you learned that I visited him for seven years in a row before he made a gift that put the seminary's capital campaign over the top.

It would probably be more accurate to say that the gift was thirty-four years in the making, for it was thirty-four years earlier that his relationship with the seminary began. In the 1980s he and his wife made a $25,000 commitment to the seminary's Endowing for Excellence campaign to endow a scholarship in memory of their former beloved pastor. Thus began a friendship with the seminary that continued to deepen over the next several years. In the 1990s they again played an important role in the seminary's Bold Leaders for a New World campaign by making a $250,000 commitment.

When the seminary launched its sesquicentennial campaign Forging Our Future in 2003, they agreed to serve as honorary cochairs and to make the lead gift—$5 million—to the campaign. When the campaign goal was raised from $35 million to $60 million in 2006, they made an additional $5 million commitment. The goal was again raised to $100 million in 2009, which is when Ernie gave me a "definite maybe" when asked if he could again set the pace for this expanded goal. It was a very happy surprise when I finally received a phone call telling me that he and his wife were making another commitment of $5 million to put the campaign over the top.

In making this commitment, Ernie stated, "Truly it is our honor to help this great organization. The seminary's mission fits perfectly with ours. God has blessed us with many gifts. We in turn would like to bless others, and so it is our pleasure to support the seminary's mission." A statement like that reflects a relationship that has developed over many years.

One of the most humbling honors I ever received was when Ernie's widow asked me to officiate at his memorial service less than two years after that magnificent gift. I will forever treasure our collaborative efforts to strengthen an institution we both came to love. His legacy lives on at the seminary.

What can we learn from these happy surprises experienced over the course of thirty-four years? Successful fundraisers seek to build long-term relationships with their donors. It's as simple—and challenging—as that.

Notes

35 Dream Big Dreams

"Dream no small dreams, for they have no power to move the hearts of men," wrote German author and statesman Johann Wolfgang von Goethe. Jerre is a strong believer in that statement. He always encouraged me to dream big dreams because they inspire other people. And he dreamed big dreams himself—often resulting in happy surprises for the seminary!

When we began planning our Forging Our Future campaign in honor of the seminary's 150th anniversary, a number of people secretly wondered if a $35 million goal might be difficult to reach. Jerre was not one of them.

Jerre was named cochair of the campaign, and at the public launch he surprised many by announcing that he was making a $1.2 million gift to help kick it off. Then he surprised me by saying to all those gathered, "And when we reach $35 million, we are going to raise the goal to $50 million!"

Jerre came up to me after the speech and said, "I don't know what possessed me to say that." All I could say in response was, "I don't either!"

Just as Jerre expected, we reached the $35 million goal right on schedule. But the campaign goal was not raised to $50 million. Rather, with Jerre's encouragement, the trustees voted to raise the goal to $60 million—$10 million more than Jerre had originally suggested.

That goal was also met—three years ahead of schedule! Luckily, the goal was reached just as the economy was tanking. Jerre, however, was undeterred by the worst economy since the Great Depression. At the next board meeting, he told the trustees that Garrett-Evangelical needed to continue to run its fundraising race.

"We have reached our $60 million goal," he said, "but we still have $19 million in deferred maintenance, we still need to provide more scholarship support, we still need to endow more faculty positions, and we still need to increase our unrestricted endowment."

> **Find people who dream big. Work with them and learn from them.**

Then he surprised the board with an amazing offer. "Here is my proposal," he said. "I will make an additional $5 million commitment to this campaign if the board as a whole matches this commitment and raises the goal to $100 million!"

How would you have voted if you had been on the board? Not wanting to turn down a $5 million gift, the trustees voted unanimously to accept his challenge. The new goal was now almost three times the original goal.

Midway through this historic new campaign goal, Jerre again surprised the board by announcing that he was making an additional commitment of $9 million to the seminary's unrestricted endowment. This commitment, the largest in the seminary's history, brought the campaign total to $88 million and helped propel the campaign toward the finish line. Not too long thereafter, the $100 million goal was surpassed—a year ahead of schedule!

What can we learn from Jerre and these happy surprises? Find someone who dreams big for your team, and then work with that individual and learn from her or him!

Notes

Laugh at Life—And Especially at Yourself

I take my work seriously, but I try not to take myself too seriously. My fundraising colleagues still laugh at an incident that happened to me several years ago. And while I did not find it funny at the time, I also chuckle when I reflect on it today.

Elizabeth, one of our older alums, had sent in a request for further information on gift annuities. When I called her to answer her questions, she said she would rather visit in person and wondered if I ever got to Washington, DC. I told her I rarely got there, but I would be happy to come and see her if that would be helpful. She said she had taken out a significant gift annuity with her undergraduate alma mater several years earlier and was considering doing something similar for the seminary.

I decided it was worth visiting her, so I traveled to Washington, DC. When I arrived at her apartment complex, she was waiting for me in the lobby. I suggested we go to her apartment, where we could visit, but she insisted that we sit in the main lobby area, next to the switchboard operator. I learned about her career working at American embassies throughout the world. I also learned that, at age ninety, she was very hard of hearing.

And so I found myself trying to discreetly ask her about her estate plans in the midst of this noisy, very public setting. I'm sure she couldn't hear most of what I said.

Elizabeth finally agreed to walk next door to a restaurant, where there would be a bit more privacy. As we got up to leave, she turned to the switchboard operator and, in a stage whisper loud enough for the whole world to hear, said, "I can't get rid of him. He is so boring!" I will conclude on that note, before you say the same thing! And no, she didn't take out a gift annuity either!

Notes

Conclusion

You've heard me mention happy surprises many times throughout this book. This is not a phrase I choose lightly. Rather, for me it is a theological statement. I firmly believe that if we do our work well, God rewards our efforts with happy surprises!

And what is the work we are called to do? It is not to convince people to do something they don't want to do, or to extract a gift from an unwilling donor. Rather, it is to plant seeds (seeds of awareness about our organization's mission) and then to cultivate, nurture, and at the appropriate time harvest those seeds that mature.

I grew up on a farm, and one of my favorite parables is the parable of the sower. We are reminded that some seeds fall on rocky ground, some seeds fall on thorny ground, and some seeds fall on good soil. The sower does not cause the seeds to grow. The sower simply plants the seeds, knowing that God will cause some to grow and bring forth grain, some a hundredfold, some sixty, and some thirty. (See Matthew 13:1–23.)

And so it is with us. We are called to diligently plant seeds day in and day out. We never know for sure which seeds will sprout and produce gifts, some a hundredfold, some sixty, and some thirty. We simply know that if we are faithful in our work, the Word is our promise, and we can rest in the knowledge that God will cause some seeds to grow and bring forth grain. These are our happy surprises—and they never fail to delight because they remind us that God is always at work in our midst.

There is a hymn entitled "What Gift Can We Bring." Verse 3 summarizes well my own theology, and I conclude with its words:

Give thanks for tomorrow, full of surprises,
for knowing whatever tomorrow may bring,
the Word is our promise, always, forever;
we rest in God's keeping and live in God's love.
Amen.

About the Author

David Heetland served as vice president for development at Garrett-Evangelical Theological Seminary in Evanston, Illinois, for thirty-five years. During that time the seminary consistently ranked as one of the top seminaries in the nation in dollars raised and in percentage of alums supporting the institution. Under his leadership the seminary successfully completed three major capital campaigns, including the most successful capital campaign in the seminary's history, Forging Our Future, which raised more than $100 million and was completed a year ahead of schedule. In July 2018 he became senior vice president for planned giving. In his new role he works with people who wish to help the seminary fulfill its mission through estate planning.

Before coming to Garrett-Evangelical, Heetland served at Dakota Wesleyan University in Mitchell, South Dakota, for six years, first as campus minister and assistant professor of religion and philosophy, then as dean of students, and finally as vice president for institutional advancement. He began his ministry serving as a church pastor for two years.

Dr. Heetland has lectured at a number of national gatherings, including several national seminars for development officers in theological education. He has authored a book, *Fundamentals of Fund Raising: A Primer for Church Leaders* (Nashville: Discipleship Resources, 1989), and edited another, *Seminary Development News: The First Ten Years* (D. Heetland, 1996). He has also published numerous articles, book reviews, and sermons that have appeared in such publications as *The Chronicle of Philanthropy, Fund Raising Management,* and *The Christian Century.* For ten years he edited *Seminary Development News,* a quarterly newsletter sent to all seminaries in the United States and Canada. He is a frequent preacher, speaker, and consultant to various nonprofit organizations.

Dr. Heetland holds a BA from the University of South Dakota; an MDiv and a ThD from Iliff School of Theology in Denver, Colorado; and a diploma in theology from Cambridge University in Cambridge, England. He is also a Certified Financial Planner. He and his wife, Kathy, a professional musician, have two grown daughters, two sons-in-law, and five grandchildren.